HOLD THAT THOUGHT

Sarah Ban Breathnach

Illustrations by Margaret Chodos Irvine

WARNER ⦿ TREASURES®
PUBLISHED BY WARNER BOOKS
A TIME WARNER COMPANY

Simple Abundance®
is a registered trademark of Sarah Ban Breathnach

Warner Treasures® name and logo are
registered trademarks of Warner Books, Inc.
1271 Avenue of the Americas
New York, NY 10020
🆆 A Time Warner Company

Visit us at our Web site: http://www.pathfinder.com/twep

Printed in Singapore
First printing: March 1997
10 9 8 7 6 5 4 3 2 1
ISBN: 0-446-91207-7

Calendar design by Diane Luger
Calendar Illustrations by Margaret Chodos Irvine

This year I want you to become aware that you already possess all the inner wisdom, strength, and creativity needed to make your dreams come true. This is hard for us to realize because the source of this unlimited personal power is buried so deeply beneath the bills, the car pool, the business trip, and the dirty laundry that we have difficulty accessing it in our daily lives. When we can't access our inner resources, we come to the flawed conclusion that happiness and fulfillment come only from external events. That's because external events usually bring with them some sort of change. And so we've learned to rely on circumstances outside ourselves for forward or backward momentum as we hurtle through life. But we don't have to do that. We can learn to be the catalysts for our own change.

At the heart of Simple Abundance is an authentic awakening, one that resonates within your soul; all you have is all you need to be genuinely happy. The way you reach that awareness is through an inner journey that brings about an emotional, psychological, and spiritual transformation. A deep inner shift in your reality occurs, aligning you with the creative energy of the Universe. Such change is possible when you invite Spirit to open the eyes of your awareness to the abundance that is already yours.

Six principles will guide us as we make our inner journey over the next year. These are the six threads of abundant living which, when woven together, produce a tapestry of contentment that wraps us in inner peace, well-being, happiness, and a sense of security. First there is *gratitude*. When we do a mental and spiritual inventory of all that we have, we realize that we are very rich indeed. Gratitude gives way to *simplicity*—the desire to clear out, pare down, and realize the essentials of what we need to live truly well. Simplicity brings with it *order*, both internally and externally. A sense of order in our life brings us *harmony*. Harmony provides us with the inner peace we need to appreciate the beauty that surrounds us each day, and *beauty* opens us to *joy*. But just as with any beautiful needlepoint tapestry, it is difficult to see where one stitch ends and another begins. So it is with Simple Abundance.

In my experience, when going down for the third time, it was often word-to-word resuscitation that saved the day. That's why I've gathered some of my favorite Simple Abundance thoughts to remind you that each day is a new gift. In this calendar may you find moments of comfort, glimmers of joy and a deep awareness of the "simple abundance" that surrounds us all. Blessings on your journey to Wholeness.

Sarah Ban Breathnach
Sarah Ban Breathnach

New Year's Day. New questions to
be asked and embraced. Answers to be
discovered, then lived in this transformative
year of delight and self-discovery.

DECEMBER 31

Once you accept and rejoice in your authenticity, you begin to see things as YOU are. You begin to see the authentic self is the Soul made visible. Godspeed on your journey to Wholeness.

*Only dreams
give birth to change.*

Believe. Believe in yourself. Believe in the One who believes in you. All things are possible to she who believes. Blessings on your courage.

Take a leap of faith and begin this wondrous new year by believing. Believe in yourself. Believe that there is a loving Source—a Sower of Dreams—just waiting to be asked to help make your dreams come true.

DECEMBER 29

Today is not the day you quit. Nor is it the day you cry. Today you know that you have all the passion and wisdom to find that quiet center of solace, serenity, and strength necessary to create and sustain an authentic life.

None of us can be expected to perform every minute of our lives. But a lot of us might tap into the power, excitement, and glory of Real Life more frequently if we cast ourselves as the leading ladies in our own lives.

DECEMBER 28

This is not the time you stop believing.
You simply can't afford the luxury of skepti-
cism. In the past a woman's spirituality has
been separated from her lifestyle. But now
you know this doesn't make any sense.
Never did. Never will.

Turn away from the world this year.
Look within. Your authentic self has lit
lanterns of love to illuminate the path to
Wholeness. At long last, the journey
you were destined to take has begun.

As the season of believing seems to wind down let me gently remind you that many dreams still wait in the wings. Many authentic sparks must be fanned before passion performs her perfect work in you. Throw another log on the fire.

*How many of us go through our days
parched and empty, thirsting after happiness,
when we're really standing knee-deep in
the river of abundance?*

DECEMBER 26

"Life University" has two classes: "Heaven on Earth" and "Seminar on Understanding the Mechanics of How Heaven Works." The first is a Real Life work/study program. The second is an intellectual seminar on how to try to manipulate real life, with a little metaphysical mumbo jumbo.

Choose today to quench your thirst
for "the good life" you think others lead by
acknowledging the good that already exists in
your own life. Then offer the Universe
the gift of your grateful heart.

It has been said many times that our lives are gifts from God—that what we do with them is our gift in return. Today is the perfect day to remember this.

*It is difficult to experience moments
of happiness if we are not aware of what
it is we genuinely love.*

Christmas won't be Christmas without any gifts. How about unconditional Love? Trust. Second Chances. Comfort. Joy. Wonder. Acceptance. Courage. To give such gifts. To truly open our hearts to receive such gifts gratefully.

Your happiness is not a frivolous, expendable luxury. But you have to be willing to pursue it. Ultimately, genuine happiness can only be realized once you commit to making it a priority in your life.

The Holy Grail is our authenticity. It's glimpsed hidden among what is familiar to us—home, family, work, pleasures.

JANUARY 10

If you are to live happily, creatively,
and with a sense of fulfillment, it is crucial to
distinguish between your wants and your
needs. When you blur the distinction, it's
no wonder you feel so diminished.

DECEMBER 22

*It doesn't matter whether we reflect
the Light through our authentic gifts or
whether our authentic calling is to spread it.
Tonight the world is dark but your flame burns
brightly. Share it with others. Watch
the Light return.*

JANUARY 11

*Make peace with the awareness
that you can't have everything you want.
It's more important for you to get everything
you need. Contentment comes when our
essential needs are met.*

DECEMBER 21

In the natural world, winter is the season of rest, restoration, and reflection. There's not much of that going on this week, but after the holidays are over, consider how you spend whatever time you have at your personal disposal.

Lasting change does not happen overnight. Lasting change happens in infinitesimal increments: a day, an hour, a minute, a heartbeat at a time.

Deliberate visualization over a period of time usually results in the desired end. The subconscious mind sets in motion whatever behavior and circumstances are necessary to manifest physically the desired program.

Worries about money mock you. They steal the joy of living. When you worry about money you dread the days and agonize at night. You cease to live and merely exist.

DECEMBER 19

Visualizations are daydreaming's virtual reality: a deliberate, positive scene-setting of what you'd like to see happen in your future. Our visualizations should be so realistic they trigger an emotional response: happiness, ecstasy, relief, thanksgiving.

If you are worried about money, take heart.
You have the power to move from a feeling of
lack to one of abundance. Money ebbs and flows;
what should remain constant is the realization
that abundance is your spiritual birthright.

Daydreams are the fertile soil in which our imaginations flourish and reach for the Light. Daydreams incubate creativity and make possible reveries, visualization, and maybe even visions.

The simpler we make our lives, the more abundant they become. There is no scarcity except in our souls.

DECEMBER 17

*Naps help us sort, sift, separate the
profound from the profane, the possible
from the impossible. If you want to be happy
for the rest of your life, napping
is not optional.*

*Today surrender your desire for security
and seek serenity instead. When you do, you
will look at your life with new eyes.*

We're emotional drunks when we
binge on the self-abuse of raging and crying
for hours. Tantrums leave us exhausted,
unable to receive or give love.

How much abundance that already exists in your life do you take for granted? How can we expect more from the Universe when we don't appreciate what we already have?

DECEMBER 15

Many women today are struggling with addictions to drink, drugs, smoking, food, sex, shopping, or sleeping. But there's another "habit" that affects many but gets little airplay: addiction to the highs and lows of emotions.

Gratitude is the first step on the Simple Abundance path or it just won't work. Simplicity, order, harmony, beauty, and joy—all the other principles that can transform your life will not blossom and flourish without gratitude.

You would be astounded at the relief that comes once you stop assuming you have all the answers.

When we appreciate how much we have, we feel the urge to pare down, get back to basics, and learn what is essential for our happiness. We long to realize what's really important.

Most of us operate under the assumption that daily life is a one-woman battleground. It's no wonder we're amazed when out of the blue, the Force suddenly seems to be with us. Grace is the Force. Ask for today's portion.

Many believe simplicity implies doing without. But true simplicity as a conscious life choice is both buoyant and bountiful, able to liberate depressed spirits from the bondage and burden of extravagance and excess.

Grace is direct Divine intervention on our behalf that circumvents the laws of nature—time, space, the availability of parking—for our highest good. We access grace by asking for it specifically and regularly.

Less can mean more for those of us on the Simple Abundance path. Every day offers us simple gifts when we are willing to search our hearts for the place that's right for each of us.

DECEMBER 11

*The outward and visible way in which
we move through our daily round—the time,
creative energy, emotion, and attention with
which we endow our tasks—is how we elevate
the mundane to the transcendent.*

When you feel overwhelmed by outside circumstances beyond your control, getting your house or even desk in order can restore your equilibrium.

DECEMBER 10

In its purest form, prayer is actually authentic conversation. You can say whatever needs to be said. You won't be judged. You won't risk losing love; instead, by praying you will increase your awareness of it.

When you can't control what's happening externally in your life, learn to look to your own inner resources for a sense of comfort that nurtures and sustains.

DECEMBER 9

Everyday life is the prayer. How we conduct it, cherish it, celebrate it, consecrate it. It's just that some prayers are better than others. Conscious prayers are the best.

If you feel constantly adrift but don't know why, be willing to explore the role that order—or the lack of it—plays in your life. No woman can think clearly when constantly surrounded by clutter, chaos, and confusion.

DECEMBER 8

Some women know they pray.
Other women think they don't because they
aren't down on their knees morning and night.
But they're up in the dark with sick children,
or helping a friend bear grief or rejoice.
This, too, is prayer.

Today begin to think of order not as a
straitjacket of "shoulds" (make the bed,
wash the dishes, take out the garbage) but
as a shape—the foundation—for the
beautiful new life you are creating.

DECEMBER 7

When you acknowledge your romantic impulses, no matter how impractical, you strengthen the intimate connection with your authentic self. Connection with those things that fuel your passions, feed your soul, keep you alive.

Usually when the distractions of daily life deplete our energy, the first thing we eliminate is the thing we need the most: quiet, reflective time. This is the definition of insanity.

DECEMBER 6

Plumb the female psyche and you will find an elegy of romantic remorse—the unobtained, the undone. Regrets not caused by a lover who chose to live without us, so much as by recollections of the things we loved once but learned to live without.

As you introduce gratitude, simplicity, and order into your life, harmony emerges. On the Simple Abundance path, you learn to balance demands with pleasures, solitude with companionship, the inner woman with the outer packaging.

Instead of worrying, consider what actions you could take to create money. Transforming every "What will I do?" into "What can I do?" fuels your fiscal creativity, restoring a sense of peace as you pursue prosperity.

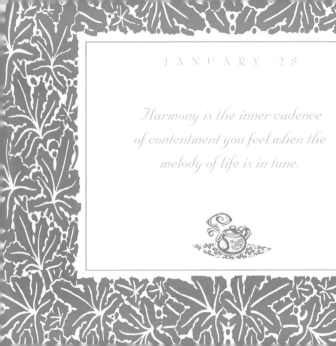

*Harmony is the inner cadence
of contentment you feel when the
melody of life is in tune.*

DECEMBER 4

Worry is a future-tense emotion. Worry is a projection of a possible—not necessarily probable—scenario. Will there be enough? Where will it come from? How long will it last? Worry is wasteful.

Let today be an adagio—a melody played in an easy, graceful manner. Play soothing, uplifting music; while you listen, consider how all the individual notes come together harmoniously to give expression to the entire score.

Anytime you have more than you need, you have abundance. Catch yourself the next time you start dwelling on what you don't have; switch tracks by noticing and appreciating all you do.

Creating a beautiful life is your highest calling. Celebrate this new awareness. It is in the details of life that beauty is revealed, sustained and nurtured.

DECEMBER 2

Worrying about money never paid a bill. If it did, at least there'd be a legitimate reason for indulging in it. Actually, worrying about money repels, rather than attracts, prosperity by sending toxic signals to the subconscious.

*Many of us unconsciously create
dramas in our minds, expecting the worst
from a situation only to have our expectations
become a self-fulfilling prophecy.*

DECEMBER 1

Comparisons hurt us in profound ways.
They undermine our confidence. Shut down
our flow of creative energy. Suck the life force
from our marrow. Coveting destroys
what is Sacred within.

Today realize you don't have to be the author of your own misfortune. Stop the dramas and start to trust the flow of life and the goodness of Spirit.

Comparisons are irresistible but insidious, and very often our self-torture of choice. Today, let's meditate on not coveting our neighbor's husband, figure, home, clothes, income, or career.

FEBRUARY 2

*Trusting an outside power to help make our
dreams come true can be threatening, especially
if we're used to being in control—or rather, used
to the illusion of being in control. Today, be
willing to believe a companion Spirit
is leading you every step of the way.*

Become abundant with your compliments to others. We're all so fragile, especially when we put on a brave face. A sincere compliment can penetrate beneath even the most sophisticated masks to soothe troubled souls.

FEBRUARY 3

Accepting our circumstances is a powerful tool for transformation. Acceptance is surrendering to what is: our feelings, our problems, the delay of our dreams. Acceptance allows the steam of struggle to escape from life's pressure cooker.

Remember, if we aren't open to
receiving good things, at some point the
Universe may no longer bother with us. No one
enjoys hanging around an ingrate, and that's
exactly what we are when we discount the
marvelous about ourselves.

FEBRUARY 4

*Before we can change anything in our
life we must recognize that this is how it's meant
to be right now. Accept your current situation.
Let go of the struggle. Mourn so that you might
move on. Allow the healing process to begin.*

Most of us feel that we deserve more compliments than we receive. But maybe we don't hear as many compliments as we'd like because whenever one has our name on it, we return it to the sender: "Oh, this old thing?" "It was nothing."

*After accepting our present circumstances,
no matter what they are, we must learn to bless
them, through gritted teeth if necessary. This
blessing is the spiritual surrender that changes
even troublesome situations for the better.*

Don't wish today away. Don't waste it.
Redeem one hour to be grateful. Let your
thanksgiving rise above the din of disappoint-
ment—opportunities lost, mistakes made, the
clamor of all that has not yet come.

Blessing the circumstances in your life teaches you to trust. If you're sick and tired of learning life's lessons through pain and struggle, blessing your difficulties will show you there's a better way.

If we are alive, we cannot escape loss. Loss is a part of real life. Today might be tough for you. But at least you have it. You still have a choice as to how you will live this precious day.

Today start to make a spiritual inventory of all your blessings. So much good happens to us but in the rush of daily life we fail even to notice or acknowledge it.

Artists of the everyday excel in
elevating the simple to the Sacred. You
can use whatever you have on hand — a meal,
a conversation, humor, affection — to create
comfort and contentment.

Life is always movement, always change, always unforeseen circumstances. So stop waiting for life to become calm and start working with what you've got to make it as satisfying as you can.

Don't feel you must deny your feelings when you want something beautiful but can't afford it. The desire offers clues to satisfy this holy hunger. Explore why you behold something as beautiful, then use your impressions to jump-start your imagination.

*The key to loving how you live is
knowing what it is you truly love. Think of
one thing that would give you a genuine
moment of pleasure today and do it.*

*For every "yes" make sure
you also say "no" to another request.*

*Our wishes for the future, our
hopes, our dreams, our aspirations are
our truest treasures. Guard yours in the
sanctuary of your heart.*

To create boundaries we must speak up. These moments can easily escalate into confrontations, which is why many women stay quiet, rendered virtually mute by unexpressed rage and unable to articulate any needs at all.

*The greatest secret to living a happy
and fulfilled life is realizing that everything
is created in our minds before it manifests
itself in the outer world. We must believe
before we can see.*

Boundaries set apart the Sacred
with simple grace. We must learn the art
of creating boundaries that protect, nurture,
and sustain all we cherish.

As we become curators of our own contentment on the Simple Abundance path, one of the great payoffs is that we start to seek peace and comfort in joyful simplicities. Little things begin to mean a lot to us.

Limits are the barbed wire of real life.
Boundaries are split-rail fences. When you
push past your limits, there's a good chance of
being pricked as you hurtle up and over. But
there's always enough room to maneuver between
the rails if you're willing to bend.

FEBRUARY 13

*Life comes together when we seek of
the sublime in the ordinary. Today make
discovering those joyful simplicities that bring
you personal comfort and a sense of well-
being one of your highest priorities.*

Like a phantom lover, work charms, cajoles, comforts, and caresses. Our work can be so seductive that we can find ourselves completely caught up in its rapture. But the ultimate seduction may bring the ultimate addictions: workaholism and perfectionism.

FEBRUARY 14

It takes great love and courage to excavate buried dreams. Today is the day set aside for love, a perfect occasion to call forth the dream you buried long ago with disbelief.

*When you have no strength left, you
have no choice but to rely on the strength
of a saner Power to restore you to Wholeness.
In the pursuit of our souls, Spirit
takes no prisoners.*

It should be straightforward, this knowing what we love. But it seldom is. Trust that your authentic path will unfold naturally and with grace.

When you're suffering from
burnout, you are the only person on
earth who can help because you're the only
one who can make the lifestyle changes that
need to be made: to call a halt, to take
a slower path, to make a detour.

FEBRUARY 16

*Making the absolute best of ourselves is
no easy task. It requires patience, persistence,
and perseverance. For many of us it also requires
prayer. It can be far easier to learn to live by our
own lights when we access a Higher Source of
Power to illuminate our path.*

It's burnout when nothing satisfies you because you haven't a clue what's wrong. You feel there is not one other person on the face of the earth who can help you.

And you're right.

When we ask for Light we see remarkably well. We see with clarity. And what we can see if we look deep within is that the authentic self is the Soul made visible.

NOVEMBER 14

*It's burnout when you can't believe,
under any circumstances, that you'll ever
want to make love again. It's burnout when
you find yourself cranky all the time, bursting
into tears or fits of rage at the
slightest provocation.*

Only when the clamor of the outside world is silenced will you be able to hear the Deeper Vibration. Listen carefully. Spirit's playing your song.

*It's burnout when you go to bed
exhausted every night and wake up tired
every morning—when no amount of sleep
refreshes you, month after weary month.
It's burnout when even going on vacation
becomes too much effort.*

Restoring a sense of rhythm to our lives is crucial to discovering Wholeness. Think of the steady, reassuring rhythm of the natural world—the tide's ebb and flow, the easing of day into night. What role does rhythm play in your daily round?

Don't think burnout only happens to other women. Careaholics are at risk—women who care deeply about their children, work, relationships, parents, siblings, friends, communities, issues. This sounds like every woman.

FEBRUARY 20

*Start thinking of yourself as an
artist and the beautiful authentic life you
are creating for yourself and those you
love as a work-in-progress.*

NOVEMBER 11

Setting the world on fire is risky, but we usually don't realize this until smoke gets in our eyes. Burnout is a condition caused by unbalance: too much work or responsibility, too little time to do it, over too long a period. Sound familiar?

Works-in-progress are never perfect.
But changes can be made to the rough draft
during rewrites. Another color can be added
to the canvas. The film can be tightened
during editing. So can life.

*The seasons of life are not
meant to be frenetic, just full. Blessed is
the woman who knows her own limits.*

FEBRUARY 22

*Most of us don't think of ourselves
as artists, but we are. An artist is merely
someone with good listening skills who accesses
the creative energy of the Universe to bring
forth something on the material plane
that wasn't there before.*

We cannot circumvent the laws of Heaven
and earth just because it would be convenient.
Just because it would fit nicely into our plans.
We have tried. We have failed.

FEBRUARY 23

Trust your instincts. Follow your yearnings.
Respect your creative urges. If you are willing
to step out in faith and take a leap in the dark,
you will discover that your choices are
as authentic as you are.

NOVEMBER 8

*You cannot raise happy, secure,
well-adjusted children, revel in a fabulous
relationship, and work a sixty-hour week.
You want to, I know. So do I. But it
is physically, emotionally, and
spiritually impossible.*

FEBRUARY 24

Having money does not guarantee that we live authentically. Nor does being surrounded by beautiful things guarantee happiness. If you receive heartbreaking news, it's not more comforting to sob into a damask and silk-tasseled cushion.

*The heart does not charge for consultations,
conversations, creative brainstorming sessions,
or carrying a dream from conception to deliv-
ery, no matter how long it takes.*

FEBRUARY 25

When you learn what you can live without,
you are able to ask life for the very best because
you possess the gift of discernment. You are able
to create an authentic life because you are
able to make conscious choices.

The heart also tells us when we've made a wrong turn or when it's time for a U-turn. For a lot of us, this is information we don't want to know. Knowing might mean choice, and choice often means change.

*Turning away from the world
and toward your own happiness is the
path of authenticity.*

Only the heart knows what's working in our lives. The heart is our authentic compass. If we consult her, the heart can tell us if we're headed in the right direction.

FEBRUARY 27

You have embarked on an adventure as exciting as any explorer's. But uncovering the source of the Nile or charting the course of the Amazon is nothing compared to the inner journey to Wholeness—a safari of the self and Spirit.

Spirit knows that the rate of exchange on earth is cash. But the rate of exchange in Heaven is wonder. Doing what you love is all about wonder. When you understand you must pursue wonder instead of money, you'll start experiencing abundance.

FEBRUARY 28

In Africa, to go on safari—the Swahili
word for journey—is to leave the comfort of
civilization to venture into the wilderness.
Each time you listen to your authentic self you
do the same. Remind yourself of this often.

When you start following your
authentic path, you're finally holding up
your end of the bargain. Spirit's part of the
pact is to make sure you have everything
you need to make you truly happy.
This includes money.

FEBRUARY 29

A safari of the self and Spirit is at times lonely. But this sense of isolation is necessary if we are to encounter Mystery, and mystery is very much a part of a safari. Embrace the Mystery of the wilderness within.

Could your bliss and an authentic
life be one and the same? What if whatever
it is that satisfies your hunger, ignites your
passion, and gives you peace—in other
words, your bliss—is also the
Kingdom of Heaven?

Believe it or not, you have lived many lives, and each has left indelible marks on your soul: childhood, early career, marriages, perhaps life alone. Each life's legacy is moments of contentment; things we've loved that when recalled, reveal glimmers of our true selves.

Spiritual seekers are told to search for the Kingdom of Heaven. Could the Kingdom of Heaven be an authentic life? I believe so. Because once you find your authentic path and follow it, all the other puzzle pieces fall into place.

MARCH 2

*Some of us are reluctant to recall
our past because we're afraid of painful
memories. But as each illness brings a gift if
we will look for it, so each painful memory comes
bearing a peace offering. Do not fear. The
past asks only to be remembered.*

OCTOBER 31

O daughter of the She, the power of Love has been gifted you. Commit to using it wisely for the Highest Good of all. You touch countless lives in your lifetime. Heal them with the magic at your command.

By paying attention to the details—
your authentic gestures—you give expression
to the most personal of all the arts: your
own imprint on life.

O C T O B E R   3 0

*Most women are not aware of
their tremendous power for good. We are
asleep to our Divinity. We've not consciously
awakened to the realization that we are
descendants of an ancient, sacred
lineage: the She.*

The details of our days
do make a difference in our lives.

*How many times have we waited
for Spirit to move for us, when in fact,
Spirit is patiently waiting to
work with us?*

How many times in the past have
we chosen not to change our lives for the
better simply by not choosing?

OCTOBER 28

*You may have believed that
seeking a spiritual path was all about
submission, sacrifice, and suffering and that
only the worldly path could provide fulfillment.
Then, one morning you make a connection.
It's the reverse.*

Reverence is that altered state of consciousness when you feel awe and wonder because you know you are in the presence of Spirit. By meditating or creating something beautiful, you can often spiritually induce this special moment of Wholeness.

OCTOBER 27

Now the revelations come very quickly because you're ready to start making connections. They might come while you are chatting casually with a friendly grocery clerk. Don't cut yourself off from sources of inspiration.

MARCH 7

Real Life—the real life of joy we are meant to be living—begins when we restore a sense of reverence to our daily affairs. Today, search for the Sacred in the ordinary with gratitude in your heart and you will surely find it.

OCTOBER 26

*The biggest surprise on the
soulful journey to authenticity, whether as
a philosophy or a spiritual path, is that the
path is a spiral. We go up, but we go in
circles. Each time around, the view
gets a little bit wider.*

Grace is available for each
of us every day—our spiritual daily
bread—but we've got to remember to ask
for it with a grateful heart and try not to
worry about whether there will be enough
for tomorrow. There will be.

OCTOBER 25

*It takes an entire lifetime to live
authentically. It is the striving to be
authentic that makes you so, not the end
result. When you think you've arrived, you
realize you've come all this way just
to begin again.*

*Simplicity gains importance in our lives as
we begin to make peace with ourselves, and
gradually come to the inner awareness that we
don't need to gild the lily. Some of the trappings
can be relinquished because the Real Thing
is finally ready to be revealed.*

All women experience ambivalence about success. One significant quality found in the women we admire is that they have identified their personal patterns of self-sabotage and learned to let their authentic self outsmart the enemy within.

To undo the damage we have done
by remaining dormant for years, we must
reconnect with our authentic selves. We must
treat ourselves gently with the kindness we
would bestow on amnesiacs who need the
patient reassurance of their true identities.

OCTOBER 23

*The worst thing about
intimidation is that she knows all
your buttons and just when
to push them.*

Let the potent power of simplicity begin to work in your life. When in doubt, live without. No more settling for something that's not you or that's second-rate.

OCTOBER 22

*Intimidation works differently
from naked fear. She's a shape changer,
capable of adopting different guises
to control you.*

As you become more intimate
with your authentic self a gradual but
undeniable physical transformation will occur.
It is absolutely impossible to awaken your own
radiant interior Light and not have it
reveal itself on the outside.

Your authentic self is your ego's worst nightmare. And the ego will do everything in its power to eliminate her rival's influence from your daily routine. To do this, the ego brings out the heavy guns: fear and intimidation.

Your first duty every day is
to love yourself into Wholeness. We
recover our authentic selves one
kind gesture at a time.

OCTOBER 20

When you become authentic,
you become greater than you ever thought
you could be, and this greatness allows
you to heal yourself, your family,
and your world.

*If you want your life to come together,
you have to start treating yourself better.
Today, make a list of ten nice things you could
do for yourself. Now select one and do it. You
have nothing to lose from experimenting with
self-nurturing and everything to gain.*

It isn't always fate that messes up your best-laid plans. Your ego has everything to lose once your authentic self begins guiding your creative choices, decisions, ambitions, and actions for your Highest Good. The ego is not a gracious loser.

You see yourself in the mirror every day.
But when was the last time you liked what you
saw? Today, try something radically different:
look at yourself lovingly and begin to appreciate what you see. I hope it's the beautiful
woman you truly are.

One thing is certain. We cannot achieve without ambition. Action—ambition in motion—is what produces achievement.

By taking time to step outside our own sphere to embrace others, we open ourselves up to the power of the Spirit. We are suddenly lit up from inside, and this illumination transforms our appearance more effectively than any fancy salon makeover.

Think of all that could be accomplished if women cherished their ambitions. Think of how our lives could be transformed if we respected ambition and gave grateful thanks for being entrusted with such a miraculous gift.

Self-confidence is a special elixir that Spirit has prepared to help each of us face and surmount the challenges of life. It's an aromatic blending of invigorating essences, attitude, experience, wisdom, optimism, and faith.

OCTOBER 16

We are supposed to be ambitious.
Our refusal to channel our ambitions for our
highest good, the highest good of those we
love and the rest of the world, is the
real corruption of power.

When you're unsure of yourself,
remember that you can always borrow a
self-confident attitude from your authentic self.
If we act as if we're confident, we become so.
At least for a little while.

What if ambition is a gift of Spirit?
What if ambition is part of the authentic
package? If sex can be both sacred and
profane, if power blesses as well as destroys,
why should the nature of ambition
be any different?

Once you search within for your own special gifts of Spirit, your material desires diminish. Your soul divests for you rather than your conscious mind.

Ambition is achievement's soul mate.
Action is the matchmaker that brings these
affinities together so that sparks can begin
to fly and we can set the world on fire.

*Simple Abundance is not about deprivation;
Simple Abundance is meditating on the comfort
and joy of moderation, as well as gentle instruction
on how to become open to receiving the
goodness of Real Life.*

In life the worst thing that
can happen isn't failing. It's never
having tried.

The Universe is not stingy. We are.
Some of us have very stingy souls. Perhaps
not in how we treat others, but in how we treat
ourselves. Yet how can Spirit give more if our
fists, hearts, and minds are clenched tight?

OCTOBER 12

Failure stretches us beyond our conscious capacity so that we can grow into our authentic selves. This is failure's generous gift.

MARCH 22

*Today declare to the Universe that you
are open to receiving all the abundance it's
waiting patiently to bestow. Each day offers us
the opportunity to learn that as well as giving,
it is blessed to receive with grace and
a grateful heart.*

OCTOBER 11

We fear success with good reason.
We've got a lot at stake. Success brings
change, and change is uncomfortable. But by
attempting to achieve one challenge at a time,
we redefine success for ourselves and
those we love.

The time has come for us to realize that until we work on increasing our self-esteem by loving ourselves in small ways, we can't begin changing ourselves for the better in big ways.

*Whether or not we like or admit it,
a woman's success is secondary to her
relationships. We fear the impact success
will have (and it most assuredly will)
not only on our own lives, but on
the lives of those we love.*

*Whatever you are waiting for—peace of
mind, contentment, grace, the inner awareness
of Simple Abundance—it will surely come,
but only when you are ready to receive
it with an open and grateful heart.*

Many women fear success much more than failure. Failure we can handle, failure feels familiar. But success means we must leave our comfort zone, the well-padded perimeter of predictability.

When in doubt, take a bath. It can calm your mind, relax your tired, tense body, and soothe your stressed soul. Baths are as necessary for spiritual replenishment and centering as are prayer and meditation.

*Although it may crown you
Queen for a Day, the world cannot confer
the recognition that will make you feel fulfilled.
Only you can. Congratulate yourself upon the
completion of a personal accomplishment.*

Skeptics make the best seekers.

*Authentic success is living
by your own lights, not by the glare
of popping flashbulbs.*

We were created to experience,
interpret, and savor the world through our
senses—our ability to smell, taste, hear, touch,
see, and intuit. Today, ask Spirit to awaken
your awareness to the sacredness of
your sensory perceptions.

OCTOBER 6

*Most of us were not taught that
there are two kinds of success: worldly and
authentic. But we need to know the difference
between what's Real and what's not, because
success is part of Life University's
required curriculum.*

Intuition is the subliminal sense Spirit endowed us with to maneuver safely through the maze that is real life. Wild animals rely on their intuition to stay alive; we should rely on ours to thrive.

OCTOBER 5

*Failure and success are the yin
and yang of achievement, the two forces in
the Universe over which we have absolutely
no control. Have you forgotten that all
you can control is your response to
failure and success?*

*We should write an elegy for every day
that has slipped through our lives unnoticed
and unappreciated. Better still, we should
write a song of thanksgiving for all the days
that remain—now that we know how
to cherish them.*

*One of the most wonderful
truths you will discover on the path
to authenticity is that your aspirations
are your possibilities.*

The soulcraft of creating and sustaining
safe havens, set apart from the world in which
we seek and savor small authentic joys,
is a sacred endeavor.

OCTOBER 3

*Remember, the longer it takes
for a dream to manifest itself, the more
comfortable you'll feel owning
your talent.*

Like it or not, the personalities of our homes are accurate barometers that reflect where we have been, what's going on in our lives, and who we are today, though not necessarily where we're heading.

OCTOBER 2

*Be extra kind to yourself
while waiting and working to make
your dreams come true.*

APRIL 1

Today—All Fool's Day—
is the perfect occasion to remember the
importance of lightening up. Lighthearted
people are closely aligned with Spirit, and
are able to receive the spontaneous
gifts that laughter brings.

OCTOBER 1

Most of the time we wait much longer for a dream to manifest itself than we ever imagined we would at its conception. That's because our concept of time and Spirit's are not the same.

APRIL 2

Today, look upon your home through the eyes
of Love. Walk around and offer thanks for the walls
and roof that safely enclose you and yours. Pause to
consider all those who have lost their homes. Be
grateful for the home you have and know
that all you have is all you truly need.

In order to hear your calling and
answer it, you must generously give yourself
the gift of time. It's not how fast you make
your dream come true, but how steadily
you pursue it.

APRIL 3

*A home's tranquillity always comes
from within no matter what the circumstances.
The space one's soul requires cannot be
measured in inches, feet, or dollars.*

Always remember, the prophetess is rarely recognized in her own household.

APRIL 4

*We are all given the choice of
reacting negatively to the demands made
on us or choosing to live abundantly. Attitude
is all. If you do not endow your life and your
work with meaning, no one will ever
be able to do it for you.*

Simply because you are pursuing your authentic calling doesn't mean the rest of the world will think it's wonderful or even worthwhile. Pay as little attention as possible to doom, doubt, and derision.

APRIL 5

Consider how caring for your home
can be an expression of your authenticity.
Creating a comfortable, beautiful, well-run
home can be among your most satisfying
accomplishments, and an illuminating
spiritual experience.

*Dreams are gifts of Spirit meant to
alter us. Trust that the same Power that
gifted you with your dream knows how to
help you make it come true.*

*In the seamless stitching
together of life, work, and art, the
thread of divine order is woven.*

How many exquisite, glorious dreams
sent to heal the world has Heaven mourned
because the dreamer, weary and discouraged,
relied only on her own strength and
could do no more?

*How you care for your home
is a subtle but significant expression of
self-esteem and can be a personal
expression of worship.*

*The closer we get to giving our dream
to the world, the fiercer the struggle becomes
to bring it forth. Why? Because we will be
inexorably changed. Of course we're scared;
we wouldn't be sane if we weren't.*

APRIL 8

*Repeat this recipe for serenity
out loud every morning and evening for
twenty-one days. "If you take it out, put it
back. If you open it, close it. If you throw
it down, pick it up. If you take it off,
hang it up."*

One of the hardest lessons we ever have
to master is accepting that all fear comes
from within, however major are the
external circumstances assaulting us.

APRIL 9

*Domestic theophanies are
visible manifestations of Spirit in
the home. We find them by looking for
Mystery in the mundane, seeing
the Sacred in the ordinary.*

If doubt, despair, and denial
threaten to dismantle your dreams today,
let Love roar up in your defense.

*Try to glimpse everything you do
in your home, no matter how insignificant
it may seem, as part of your authentic path
to Wholeness and it shall become so.*

Love will dissolve your fears by creating opportunities you couldn't have imagined before you began the search to discover and recover your authentic self.

APRIL 11

Money can purchase beautiful furnishings and decorative accessories, but it cannot ensure that charm abides with us. Charm is a quality of the soul that is accessed through your authenticity, and expressed with your personal flair.

When you start on the path to
authenticity, Love will transform you in
countless ways. Because these changes are so
small, your family and friends might not notice
at first. But you will, and you'll know that
miracles are taking place.

APRIL 12

*How much of our lives is
frittered away—spoiled, spent, or
sullied—by our neurotic insistence
on perfection?*

The price we pay for
authenticity may seem high, but who
among us can truly afford to continue
living as a spendthrift of the self?

APRIL 13

*Perfect people do not exist on
the earthly plane. Perfection leaves so
little room for improvement; so little space for
acceptance—or joy. On the path we have
chosen, progress is the simple pleasure
to be savored.*

Whether we realize it or not, there's a good reason behind everything we do or don't do, every choice we make or avoid. But we can't go forward if we don't know what's holding us back.

APRIL 14

An ancient metaphysical law says
if we desire more abundance in our lives we
must create a vacuum to allow ourselves to
receive the good we seek. We make room for
more good by giving away what we no longer
need or desire to those who do.

Some of us hear our call when we're young, but most do not because we're too busy listening to what others are telling us. So we try on different lives for size until we find one we can wear even if it doesn't necessarily fit. How well do you wear your work?

Deciding to simplify our lives and bring order to our homes by sending on the objects we no longer love to people who will genuinely appreciate them opens ourselves up to receiving an abundance that will perfectly suit us.

Most of us don't consider our work
a personal form of worship. But could there
be a more beautiful way to honor the Great
Creator than by contributing to the re-creation
of the world through our gifts?

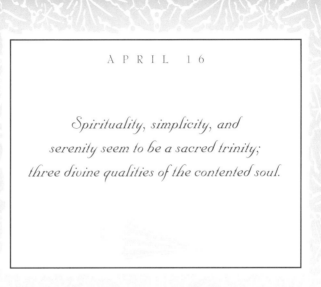

APRIL 16

*Spirituality, simplicity, and
serenity seem to be a sacred trinity;
three divine qualities of the contented soul.*

It's a mistake to accept as our reality
the illusion that many are called to fulfillment
but few are chosen. The truth is, we're all
chosen; most of us just forget to RSVP.

APRIL 17

Seek order within by book-ending your day with reflection first thing in the morning and last thing at night. The quietude will remind you that you can make the choice to live in the world but not be caught up in the frenzy of it.

Today realize that Spirit has no
hands, head, or heart like yours. No other
person on earth can do what you alone are
called to do. The call may be so faint you can
barely make out the message, but if
you listen, you will hear it.

Seeking order within means coming to grips with the craziness you've been too distracted to do anything about. When we establish order within, external order will become a visible reality in our daily round.

You don't have to run away if
you can learn to just say: enough,
enough, enough. And mean it.

APRIL 19

*When you first awaken or before drifting
off to sleep, quiet your mind, lift up your heart,
muse, mull over, make discoveries. Consider,
conceive, create, connect, concede that
it all starts within.*

Each of us was created to give outward
expression to Divinity, through our personal
gifts. Sharing our gifts with the world is our
Great Work, no matter what our job description
might be or how our resume reads.

Observe how gently but surely the natural world renews itself daily. Mother Time does not rush; seven o'clock does not tell six o'clock, "Get a move on, there are places to go, people to see, faxes to send!"

Autumnal resolutions don't require horns, confetti, and champagne. September resolutions ask only that we be open to positive change. You can do that.

No matter what our decorating style—realized or aspired to—the essential spiritual grace our home should possess is the solace of comfort.

*January resolutions are about will.
September resolutions are about authentic
wants. What do you want more or less of
in your life, so that you can love the
life you're leading?*

APRIL 22

*The search for authenticity
is like living on a fault line; you never
know when the earth is going to move
beneath your feet.*

SEPTEMBER 10

*Change in the natural world is subtle
but relentless; seasons give way gently to one
another, but the monthly motion is so swift we
don't realize we're moving. When the leaves
start turning colors, it's time to turn
over a personal new leaf.*

*Birthing a dream takes years
and exacts a price. Dreams cost money,
sweat, frustration, tears, courage, choices,
perseverance, and extraordinary patience.
But birthing a dream requires one
more thing. Love.*

Often the derailment of too many
dreams can bring on a drought. But
in the natural world, droughts depart as
suddenly and as mysteriously as they
arrive. This, too, is God.

APRIL 24

*It doesn't matter where you live at
this moment. You may be in a trailer, an
apartment, or a house—or even rooming in a
motel. Your home shelters your dreams, and
those dreams can transform any living space
into the home for which you long.*

SEPTEMBER 8

It's so difficult to come to a halt, especially when we want to get on with our careers, relationships, health, creativity. But when you're too parched to pray, or too drained to give a damn, it's time to cease and desist.

APRIL 25

*Before you pick up a hammer,
a paintbrush, or the real-estate ads, take
time to daydream. Walk through the rooms
where you eat, sleep, and live. Give thanks
as you sift and sort, simplify, and bring
order to the home you have.*

Accepting uncreative days as part of
the creative cycle is crucial to your serenity.
Uncreative days are real life. Uncreative days
are part of the yin/yang of artistic yearning.

APRIL 26

The home of your dreams
dwells within. You must find it in the
secret sanctuary of your heart today
before you can cross the
threshold tomorrow.

Hold this thought. Now say it aloud:
I am a brilliant, gifted artist of the everyday.
My art is a blessing for me and mine.

APRIL 27

The Simple Abundance path is about transformation. But transformation cannot occur without a transitional period when change is barely perceptible. The process is beneath the surface and cannot be rushed.

SEPTEMBER 5

*It takes a lifetime to create the work
of art for which we were born: an authentic
life. But it takes only minutes to offer your
love, creative energies, and enormous talents
to the person, idea, or project awaiting
your attention.*

APRIL 28

Never assume that the people in your life, especially those closest to you, won't meddle while you're on the path to authenticity. The predictable person they know is more familiar than the one they don't know, even if she/he is the Real you.

*Creation has three layers: the labor,
the craft, and the elevation. She who works
with only her hands is a laborer; she who works
with her hands and her head is a craftswoman;
she who works with her hands, her head,
and her heart is an artist.*

APRIL 29

*It's difficult to accept that emptiness
in life can be positive. We need either to
become more comfortable with waiting to fill
what's empty with what's authentic or become
just willing to accept the exquisite
fullness of nothing.*

SEPTEMBER 1

Whatever you're about to do today can
be transformed into art, if your heart is open
and you're willing to be the Great Creator's
conduit. Become an artist of the everyday.
The world does not acknowledge or applaud
everyday art, so we must.

APRIL 30

Passion is the muse of authenticity. It's the primordial, pulsating energy that infuses all of life, the luminous presence made known with every beat of our hearts.

You may not draw, paint, sculpt, knit, sing, dance, or act, but baking a cake could be as much a work of art as choreographing a ballet, if you approach it with as much dedication.

MAY 1

Passion does not reveal herself only in clandestine, bodice-ripping cliches. Passion's nature is also cloaked in the deep, subtle, quiet, and committed: nursing a baby, planting a rose garden, persevering in a dream.

The ability to bring forth art from real life is a gift each of us possesses. Whether we choose to nurture this perfectly natural endowment is quite another matter.

Every day offers opportunity
to live passionate lives rather than passive
ones, if we will stop denying ourselves pleasure.
If, as James Joyce's heroine Molly Bloom
whispered, we can learn to say ". . . and
yes I said yes I will. Yes."

AUGUST 31

*Instead of meditating today, just watch
a movie. It doesn't matter whether you choose
a home video or a bargain matinee at the mall;
truth can pleasurably be discerned one
frame at a time.*

*Passion is holy—a profound
Mystery that transcends and transforms
through rapture. We need to accept that a
sacred fire burns within, whether we're
comfortable with this truth or not.*

Finding the personal music that calls to you authentically can be empowering as you learn to nurture your creativity. Gradually build a personal collection of musical selections to help you call forth your gifts.

Passion is part of Real Life's
package because we were created by Love,
for Love, to Love. If we do not give outward
expression to our passions, we will experience
self-immolation—the spontaneous
combustion of our souls.

AUGUST 29

*Do you know that music can be a
powerful form of prayer, meditation, and
healing? Music reaches beyond the barriers
of our conscious mind and can unlock
a sense of self.*

MAY 5

*Did you know that both the
Koran, the sacred book of Islam, and
the Jewish Talmud teach that we will be
called to account for every permissible
pleasure life offered us but which we
refused to enjoy while on earth?*

AUGUST 28

*When we are frazzled, ruminating on a
line or a stanza of poetry can induce a sense of
serenity. When we allow poetry to slip slowly
beneath the sinews of our conscious mind,
connection to our authentic selves
becomes simpler.*

Let passion be your muse.
Let her guide and teach you to trust
your instincts.

AUGUST 27

Many of us squander precious natural resources—time, creative energy, emotion—comparing our talents to those of others. Today, ask Spirit to call forth your authentic gifts, so that you might know them, acknowledge them, and own them.

*It's not what you own but what
you love that expresses your authenticity.*

AUGUST 26

Sometimes the tasks we take on seem virtually impossible. But amazingly, when we harness the incredible power of the subconscious in our lives, we can accomplish whatever we set out to do, no matter what obstacles we have to overcome.

MAY 8

Meditate on modesty for a moment.
What if she isn't the self-effacing, shy,
nerdy virtue we've thought she is? What if
modesty is a virtue so full of her own
smoldering sense of self that she
isn't distracted by the glitz?

*Playing it safe is the
riskiest choice you can ever make.*

MAY 9

We want, we need, we desire, we yearn,
but we don't ask. Longings cross our mind,
but we don't really commit ourselves. But when
wishful thinking doesn't magically manifest
what we want, we feel we've been denied.

Do you want to live more abundantly?
Have you buried your talents? How can you
live more passionately if you aren't willing to
invest in yourself? Many of us have
played it safe too long and wonder
why we are miserable.

Ask for what you need and want.
Ask to be taught the right requests. Ask
for the Divine Plan of your life to unfold
through joy. Ask politely. Ask with passion.
Ask with a grateful heart and you
will be heard. Just ask.

AUGUST 23

If we don't create, we snuff out the Divine Spark. If we do create, we feel we're showing a false face to the world because we know we didn't do it alone, even if nobody else does. This illusionary scam ends, once we acknowledge the Divine Collaboration in life.

Secret anniversaries of the heart
are the anniversaries we never talk about,
kept in silence and apart. A first kiss, a
farewell. Honoring them is essential
to growing into Wholeness.

AUGUST 22

Many artists feel they'll be "found out"
sooner or later. For when we create, although
we know that a Higher Power works with us and
through us, the Work comes into the world with
our name on it. This is the artist's struggle.

How much time, creative energy, and emotion do we expend resisting change because we assume growth must always be painful? Much personal growth is uncomfortable, but it's worse to thwart the ascent of your authenticity.

AUGUST 21

*Always remember, others can imitate
but they can't duplicate your authentic gifts.*

*This is the season when growth in
the garden, which had been gradual, now
accelerates. Maybe today you'll realize that
remaining tight in the bud is more
painful than blossoming.*

Once you accept an artistic assignment from the Great Creator, it's yours. Nobody can take it away from you, unless you relinquish it. Nobody can duplicate your work because there's no one in the world like you.

Abundance and lack exist simultaneously in our lives. When we choose not to focus on what is missing but on the abundance that's present—love, health, family, friends, work—the wasteland of misery falls away and we experience daily joy.

AUGUST 19

Why do we make ourselves sick competing against others? It's just another sophisticated, seditious form of self-sabotage. If we don't measure up, why even try?

Today tend your interior
secret garden. Weed out disappointments,
frustrations, and anger; these emotional weeds
only choke your creativity. Let an unfettered
imagination sow the seeds of possibility in
the rich soil of your soul.

One reason many of us have trouble bringing our work into the world is that unconsciously we're competing instead of creating, which always short-circuits the flow of inspiration. The fault line of comparison runs deep.

MAY 16

*Being a late bloomer means that you
have the opportunity to revise and revamp
if you experiment with life and fall short of your
dreams. Late bloomers can risk more because
by now nobody really expects anything
spectacular from us.*

AUGUST 17

"Ever tried? Ever failed? No matter,"
the Irish playwright Samuel Beckett tells us.
"Try again. Fail again. Fail better." Failure is
crucial to the creative process. Authentic
success arrives only after we have
mastered failing better.

*If we are to flourish as creative
beings, if we are to grow into Wholeness, we
must bloom wherever we are planted.*

AUGUST 16

Dare yourself to believe in your creativity, wherever it may lead you. Trust that where it leads is exactly where you're supposed to be. Your authentic self knows where you're headed. Don't wrestle with Spirit. Collaborate with It.

MAY 18

*You might not have the perfect career,
home, or relationship. Few of us do. But with
the gift of today, you've got another chance to
make circumstances as perfect as it's possible
to do with the resources you have.*

What if the person who wrestles with God but doesn't live to tell the tale is the one who refuses to create—a work of art, an authentic life? What if the fatal wound, the one from which we never recover, is regret?

Do you need to reconsider re-potting
for growth? How will you know? When you
have absolutely nothing in the next twenty-four
hours to look forward to. When this happens,
week in, week out, you need to realize
that you're pot-bound.

*In order to be true to a creative work,
the artist must journey to the center of the self.
Past the conscious sentries in the brain, beyond
the barbed wire barricades of the heart, into
the trenches of "truth or dare."*

MAY 20

Re-potting doesn't mean you have to leave
the relationship or quit the job. It just means
you need to gently loosen the soil around your
soul; discover what quickens your pulse, brings
a smile or a giddy lilt to your conversation.

AUGUST 13

Perhaps one of the reasons we fear excavating our authentic selves or encountering the inner artist is because creativity seems too risky. It's safer to dabble. No one really expects a dilettante to deliver the goods.

When your roots are stunted, gently untangle them with simple joys that reveal Spirit's seamless thread of mystery. Leaf. Stem. Root. Mind. Body. Soul.

AUGUST 12

*Spirit speaks to you constantly throughout
the day. You may experience a hunch, perk up
at the suggestion of a friend, or follow an urge to
try something new on a whim. Today, tune in
to the higher harmonic frequency.*

More often than we'd like to
admit, life has a way of hitting us where it
hurts. Our souls become broken fields, plowed
by pain. Often if we don't prune away the
stress and plow under the useless in
our lives, pain will do it for us.

AUGUST 11

*Many of us have unconsciously
erected barriers to protect ourselves from
failing or succeeding. We may think we're
protecting ourselves by denying our creative
impulses, but all we're doing is burying
our authentic selves alive.*

Pain prunes the unessential emotions,
ambitions, and illusions, teaching us the
lessons we either consciously or unconsciously
refuse to be taught by joy.

*The world needs your
gift as much as you need to give it.*

Pain is a wretched gardener.
Her cuts stun and sting. But pain prunes
the insignificant details that distract us
from what is really important.

AUGUST 9

*Once you begin to nurture
Divinity's dream—with your creativity,
devotion, emotion, intelligence, passion, skill,
and tears—you will grow into your talent.
You'll be astonished at what the Great
Artistic Alliance accomplishes.*

MAY 25

One way or another our boughs will
be shaped and strengthened. Study your
lifestyle. When the right moment arrives, go
into the inner garden with sharp shears.
Speak kindly. Pray softly. Prune back.
Now plow ahead.

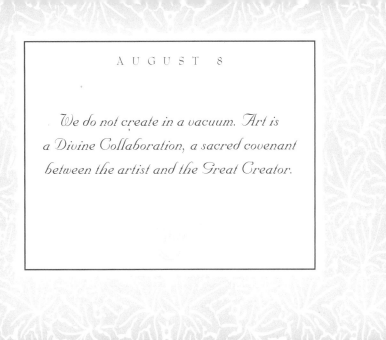

AUGUST 8

We do not create in a vacuum. Art is a Divine Collaboration, a sacred covenant between the artist and the Great Creator.

MAY 26

*Study the cycles of Mother Nature,
for they correspond with the cycles of your
soul's growth. Quiet your mind. Rope in the
restlessness. Be here. Learn to labor. Learn
to wait. Learn to wait expectantly.*

*Don't worry that your talent won't
be adequate to the task. Actually feeling
inadequate to the task you're asked to do
seems to be a spiritual prerequisite.*

The garden teaches us lessons about
sowing and reaping, as well as seedtime and
harvest. Whatever you sow, you will reap. If you
sow only positive seeds in your subconscious—
thoughts of plenty and not of lack—you
will harvest abundance.

AUGUST 6

*Few are immune to the
opinions of others. We need to learn
how to dispassionately assess advice: if it
is insightful, retain it. If it's
discouraging, let it go.*

The spiritual time continuum is not the same as time experienced on the earthly plane. Be patient. A year for us is a second in the spiritual dimension. This explains why an artist who has toiled for twenty years suddenly becomes an "overnight" success.

AUGUST 5

Second thoughts have aborted more dreams than all the difficult circumstances fate could ever throw you. Undermining your authenticity by succumbing to someone else's second thoughts is a sinister, subtle, and seductive form of self-abuse.

*Just as negative addictions sneak up on us
a day at a time, so do positive cravings.
Meditating, creative movement, moments of
self-nurturance that bring contentment—all
can become positive habits of well-being.*

AUGUST 4

*Please be careful about confiding
your sacred dreams. Never seek anybody's
advice if you even suspect you know what
they'll say, unless they unconditionally
support you.*

MAY 30

Today, consider the desires that really count—what you really need to be content. Then make sure there's at least three moments today that fulfill mind, spirit, and body with what you alone must have.

AUGUST 3

*The Great Creator does not
play favorites; each of us came into
being to carry on the re-creation of
the world through our gifts.*

No matter what your circumstances,
today will be as hard as you make it. Or as
pleasant. It's always our choice. Not
necessarily to like whatever life throws at us,
but at least to try to catch the ball.

AUGUST 2

*You long to call forth your gifts.
To explore your talents. To discover and
recover your creativity. But where do you
begin? You begin by offering an open
heart and a willingness to serve.*

JUNE 1

*Many of us stuff our desires down
deep into the self, as if sheer determination
can keep the lid on longing. But hunger is
holy. We're meant to be hungry and to
satisfy that hunger every day.*

AUGUST 1

*Commit to discovering,
acknowledging, appreciating, owning,
and honoring your personal gifts.*

JUNE 2

Our souls know many different kinds
of hunger: physical, psychic, emotional,
creative, and spiritual. We have been given
the gift of distinguishing among them.

Love wants, wishes, and wills nothing less than your unconditional happiness, harmony, Wholeness. This includes your work.

JUNE 3

Don't despise desire. Within your desire is the spark of the Divine. Spirit desires to be loved. You were created with lusty appetites to satisfy that longing.

*Discerning our personal gifts
is essential if we are to experience
harmony in our lives.*

J U N E   4

Love. Hunger. Appetite.
Desire. Holiness. Wholeness. It is all One.

Animals are our spiritual companions, living proof of a simply abundant source of Love. None of us need feel alone. And if there is a gift, then surely, there must be a Giver.

To be happy, should we consciously and continually strive for more accomplishments and accumulations? Or do we lower our expectations, and learn to be content with what we have? Many think that lowered expectations mean surrendering our dreams. They're wrong.

Let Mother Nature nurture today.
Take off your shoes and feel the earth beneath
your feet. Bend over a blossom and
breathe in the fragrance.

JUNE 6

Dreams and expectations are very different.
Dreams require trusting in Spirit to hold the net,
so that you can continue in the world's re-creation.
Expectations are the emotional investment the ego
makes in a particular outcome: exactly what must
happen to make that dream come true.

For a simply abundant day of bliss, give
yourself a restorative gift: sacred idleness.
You need an unexpected melodic day of
undoing to balance the discordant
days of doing too much.

The ego's expectations are never vague: Oscars, gold medals, the New York Times best-seller list. But requiring your dreams to manifest just as the ego imagines is self-destructive. For if we don't live up to the ego's expectations, we've failed again.

*"If you feel you spend too many days
accomplishing little or nothing, keep a
"What I've Done" list for a week. You may
discover that you do a bit more than you
realize— or give yourself credit for.*

*The passionate pursuit of dreams
sets your soul soaring; expectations that
measure the dreams' success tie
stones around your soul.*

JULY 23

It's not so much what we actually
have to do in any one week that kills us,
it's thinking about all we have to do. Stop
thinking and write it down.

Don't just lower your expectations. If you truly want to live a joyous and adventurous life, you should relinquish them.

When we are open to, and grateful for, gentle lessons they will arrive: laughing at our foibles and frailties; observing how our pets live so contentedly in the present; focusing on the good; and realizing what a wonderful life you're living — sooner rather than later.

JUNE 10

Dreaming, not expecting, allows Spirit to step in and surprise you with connection, completion, consummation, celebration. Dream. Show up for work. Then let Spirit deliver your dream to the world.

JULY 23

If we are willing to learn our lessons
gently, they patiently await us in countless
ways. Today, try listening to the wisdom of
a child, accepting the kindness of a friend,
reaching out to those in need, acting
on your intuition.

JUNE 11

Pursue your dream with passionate intensity and act as if its success depends entirely on you. But once you've done your best, try to let go. Have no expectations about how your work will be received. Choose to be surprised by joy.

JULY 22

All of us know about learning life's
lessons through pain, struggle, and loss.
But few of us realize that it is often the gentlest
lessons that teach us most. Serendipity can
instruct us as much as sorrow.

Dream. Do. Detach.

When we follow our authentic path with love, embracing our creative impulses, we live our truth even if what we think we're doing is just cooking a meal, nurturing a Child, sewing a curtain, or closing a deal.

JUNE 13

Tonight, think of dinner as an opportunity to jump-start your creativity, not just as another obligation. Cooking is one of the best ways for your authentic self to remind your conscious self that you are an artist.

JULY 20

What if "original sin" is denying instead
of celebrating your originality?

*If something is perplexing you
at the moment, see the situation as simply
an ingredient in the great recipe that's
Real Life. Each ingredient makes its own
authentic contribution to the whole.*

It's never too late to reclaim
your individual gifts, resuscitate a dream,
create an authentic life.

JUNE 15

Never discount the transformative
power of the fire that burns in your soul,
the water of your sweat and tears, and every
breath you take as you struggle to master
the art and unravel the mystery
of an authentic life.

JULY 18

Each of us possesses an exquisite,
extraordinary gift: the opportunity to give
expression to Divinity on earth through
our everyday lives.

JUNE 16

The good life does not depend on extravagant indulgences. Focus on the good at hand—a good glass of wine, a beautiful sunset, a loving relationship. Poverty is always experienced in the soul before it is felt in the pocket.

JULY 14

Often when we stew, we think we're doing something positive about the problem: at least we're thinking about it. But stewing can ruin an entire day — for ourselves and those in our vicinity.

JUNE 17

*Let your dinner be the highlight
of the day. If the day has been pleasurable
it's time to celebrate. If the day has been
difficult and discouraging, it's time for comfort
and consolation—blessings by themselves
and reason to celebrate.*

Are you a worrier? We all are to a certain extent, but some of us are more pessimistic than others. Worrying is a great thief of time, robbing you of the present moment.

JUNE 18

*The rituals of nourishment cry out for the
communion cups, the special plates on which to
break bread, the candle flame, the circle drawn
in the dirt. Ritual protects and heals, symbol-
izing to all who come to your table that they
are within a sacred space.*

JULY 12

Nothing that ever made you happy is ever lost. A golden thread of pleasure runs through your life. You just need to rediscover this thread before the joy of living completely unravels.

JUNE 19

You may think you're only laying a place at the supper table, but when you trust and follow your creative impulses to bring forth something beautiful, you experience the Sacred in the ordinary.

The writer Brenda Ueland tells us
that our imaginations need "moodling"—
long, inefficient, happy idling, dawdling, and
puttering—to flourish. Today make time
for some "moodling."

*When you take extra moments to prepare
an attractive table, you're really performing
an invocation, welcoming Spirit to be present.
Choosing to dine rather than just eat is a small
but significant step toward self-nurturance,
and one to savor as long as we live.*

Once we begin embarking on solitary sojourns to become reacquainted with our authentic selves, we usually discover that something is missing. It's called zest, *joie de vivre*, or "the love of life." When was the last time you reveled in something you loved?

Company is coming for dinner tonight. Guess who? Prepare to have your authentic self grace your table. Serve up generous portions of love, respect, and a hearty welcome on the most beautiful plate you own.

JULY 11

And for those days when you don't
have a moment to take care of yourself, take
to heart the advice of photographer Minor
White: "No matter how slow the film, Spirit
always stands still long enough for the
photographer It has chosen."

JUNE 22

The joy of seasonal cooking is the simplest of pleasures, but one of the most overlooked. It brings harmony and rhythm to our days, demonstrating with gentle wisdom that simplicity and abundance are soul mates.

Take comfort in knowing that
even stolen moments of solitude eventually
can add up to a lifetime of serenity. Don't
expect too much too soon, especially when
rearranging your schedule means dealing
with the expectations of others.

JUNE 23

Summer is when Mother Nature shows off, proving that the Universe is not stingy. Gardens and farmers' markets overflow with the goodness of the earth. The joy of seasonal foods transforms even ordinary days at the table into hallowed moments.

*Once we learn to accept and cherish
our need for solitude, opportunities will arrive
in which we can learn to nourish our imaginations and nurture our souls.*

JUNE 24

How often in our lives do we still not get it? The "it" could be a power struggle in an important relationship or an inability to control credit-card spending. The "it" doesn't matter. But it doesn't have to be "déjà vu" happening all over again—not if we start paying attention.

JULY 9

*It is impossible to experience
solitude regularly without authentic
passions surging forth. Solitude cracks open
the door that separates two worlds:
the life you lead today and the life
you yearn for so deeply.*

When we don't get it, it's usually because we can't process the outward experience inwardly. So we either assume that the outward manifestation is reality, or we keep repeating the experience until the familiarity of it starts to make sense.

*We don't have to make
ourselves sick before we call a psychic
time-out. Unfortunately for many women, it
is only when we do get sick that we allow
ourselves a dispensation for time
and space alone.*

JUNE 26

The language of the heart is longing;
the language of the mind is rationalizing; the
language of emotions is feeling. Spirit speaks
them all. When was the last time you had an
authentic conversation?

The surest way to hear the
soft strains of harmony is in the Silence.

JUNE 27

*Have you convinced yourself that
you don't have time for personal pursuits that
bring you contentment if they take longer than
fifteen minutes? No time to be passionate, you
have to be practical. Oh, really? Who says?*

Deliberately seeking solitude—
quality time spent away from family and
friends—may seem selfish. It is not. Solitude
is as necessary for our creative spirits to
develop and flourish as are sleep
and food for our bodies.

*Perhaps we don't hear the whispers
of authentic longing because we don't want
to hear. If we hear, we might have to
acknowledge, even respond.*

Too many of us approach time alone
as if it were a frivolous luxury rather than
a creative necessity. Why should this be so?
Could it be that by shortchanging ourselves,
the only thing impoverished
is our inner life?

JUNE 29

Today put your essential uncompromising longings on your list of priorities. Notice I did not say, "at the top." I just want to get you on your list.

*The soulcraft of devoutly caring for
our authentic selves by carving out time for
rewarding reveries rarely comes naturally.
But with practice, with patience, with
perseverance, it does come.*

JUNE 30

Space and time to nurture our creativity
are authentic hungers. Food, drink, work, sex,
shopping, or pills can reduce the gnawing to a
dull throb. But maybe if we took an hour a day
to paint, to plot, or to throw pots we wouldn't
be in pain—physical or psychic.

It's during our expectant hours—those that might once have been called "idle"—that we are most pregnant with our potential.

Explorers call our heart's
destination "true north." If you think your
true north is enough money to control your own
creative destiny, realize that we always control
our own creative destiny, though not
always its course.

We must be willing to court
contentment every step of the way on our
journey to Wholeness. For after all, the journey
is really all most of us will ever know. Day in,
day out. The journey is real life.